Anyone can write clever; the really clever thing is to write simple.

Jule Styne

You'd never know it,
But Buddy I'm a kind of poet
And I've gotta lotta things to say.
And when I'm gloomy,
You've simply gotta listen to me,
Until it's talked away…

Johnny Mercer
One For My Baby

BLAME YESTERDAY

A Broadway Suite

- by -

Donny O'Rourke

2009

ISBN 978-0-9555785-2-6

Published by Bonny Day
Glasgow

Some of these poems first appeared in
The Herald, The Scottish Review of Books,
Calliope (Branford College, Yale) and *painted, spoken.*
Others were broadcast on Santa Fe Television,
Channel 16 and BBC Radio Scotland.
Care For Another was commissioned by the Scottish Arts Council
as its poem of the month for February, 2009.
The editors responsible are most appreciatively acknowledged.

Publication supported by the
Tom Wright Memorial Trust

Credits

This book was mostly written on the terrace of my brother Stephen's house in southern Spain. I thank him for its use. An Easter Week spent as a guest of Branford College, Yale, allowed me to immerse myself in the lore and lyrics of Cole Porter and to savour the ambience of his alma mater whilst performing and reworking the material gathered here. I am indebted to Master Steven Smith and to Kristine Di Colandrea for their gracious hospitality. A major 'special recognition' bursary from the Scottish Arts Council bought me valuable time for further revision in New York. And the Scotland-Switzerland Writers' Exchange Fellowship gifted me six months of supported solitude in Bern, during which exhilarating period the collection took on its final shape. Merlin James designed the book, and counselled kindly and cannily on many aspects of this project – an artist, critic, (songwriter), and faithful friend, I owe him a great debt. Johnny Mercer said 'it takes more talent to write music, but it takes more courage to write lyrics'. I'm not so sure. Although *Blame Yesterday* may await a show tune collaborator for its full musical realisation, Edward McGuire has already (and very beautifully) set some of the lyrics as jazz 'art songs', though he has contributed much more than 'just' those beguiling melodies to the venture. Where they could, David Kinloch and Richard Price, again, kept me right. My appreciation of their assistance and solidarity, and that of all who supported me in the production and publication of this volume, overflows the space available for its expression.

Playbill

Interval

Act Two

Overture

'The first requirement of a good lyric is a good tune' reckoned Alan Jay Lerner. And in general the music (like the name of the composer – Lerner was the exception) does come first; though for the pragmatic Sammy Cahn it was famously 'the phone call'. In the present instance there were no pre-existing melodies. Nor did anybody ring me. It started with the words... These lyrics aim to represent, in proportions as precise as those of a good stiff pre-theatre cocktail, an affectionately ironic critique of, infatuated homage to and respectful intellectual engagement with, the show tune tradition in American popular song. The achievement of Lorenz Hart, Cole Porter, Frank Loesser, Johnny Mercer, Yip Harburg, Ira Gershwin, Oscar Hammerstein, Dorothy Fields, Sammy Cahn and Steven Sondheim – to name, as they say, but a few – seems to me equal to that of pretty much any twentieth-century poet one can think of; and some of these 'show people' wrote the tunes too!

'It is the best of all trades, to make songs, and the second best to sing them'. Thus Hilaire Belloc – a quotation framed and hung on Johnny Mercer's writing room wall. Well, I break into song rather the way vandals break into churches; but at poetry recitals

I have always performed (most often *a capella*) the results of my collaborations with composers, giving a great deal of thought to getting the meaning across, to 'selling' the lyric, to conversing, not about, but in and through, song. To make rather a crude and reductive distinction, a 'jazz' approach to the Great American Song Book generally privileges the music over the words, with the reverse tending to be true in 'cabaret' interpretations. Unsurprisingly, perhaps, I slightly favour the latter type of delivery, though not to the point of altogether deprecating instrumental-influenced vocal 'stylings' and brassy, belted, show-stoppers. Mark Murphy, Chris Connor, Annie Ross and Kurt Elling discard not a single nuance of verbal virtuosity in their cool, free, syncopated, improvisatory explorations; and Mandy Patinkin, John Raitt, Howard Keele and Barbara Cook – scarcely squares, if reverberantly respectful in their attitude to musical theatre communication – all know how to launch a lyric with every lexical, versified delicacy of feeling intact, right towards the most vertiginous seat up there in the gods. Really great artists strike an idiosyncratically perfect balance of words and music. Nat Cole understood this as did Mel Tormé, Dick Haymes and Johnny Hartman. Tony Bennett understands it more with every passing year, opening up a new audience for old repertoire along the way. There is, it must be admitted, a good deal to be said for enjoying show tunes in the shows they come from, in context and *in situ*. But excerpts beguile too. Any 'standard' can stand alone. There are no rules. Blossom Dearie melds cabaret and jazz. Elaine Stritch combines cabaret and ringing, resonant, forty-second-street vibrato (which you can hear in the Bronx and beyond). A repertoire so redolently rich is susceptible to all these schools of performance and more. I enjoy words as music and the music of words – having my cheesecake (from Lindy's!) and eating it. Maybe the yin and yang of words and music can be heard in the complementary perspectives of the Rosses, Steve and Annie. There is, anyway, something ineffably special about the intimacy and rapt rapport possible with a huge talent in a small room and an audience of alertly avid listeners. And at revealing what a great song has to say, at confiding a lyric's secrets, Steve Ross, Andrea Marcovicci, Mary Cleere Haran, Richard Rodney Bennett and Michael Feinstein all quietly excel in their respective 'readings', each contrastingly unique and yet for the most part expressively conversational, rather than declamatory or rhetorical – thoughtfully (in every sense) sharing centre stage with the words.

The words... *Blame Yesterday*'s are those of a trouper past his prime, missing the big time. Wannabe, has-been, or never was? Is this memoir or fantasy? Even he's not sure. I have tried to heed the injunction Dick Haymes had burned onto a wooden plaque on *his* wall: 'Keep it Simple'. But this musical in monologues features a very unreliable narrator, and the 'book' weaves together two storytelling strands; a recasting in many ways of the performer's past, and a love story within a love story. The libretto is divisible between two performers or may be sung solo, according to taste, circumstances and budget. How the respective layers of lyrics relate to each other if at all, is left, not over whimsically I hope, to readerly and directorial surmise.

To say that the artists lauded above are 'inimitable' is merely to state the manifest truth. My beholden exercise in melodic talk is a tribute to them and to every cabaret performer who ever touched or even, occasionally and more deeply, moved me – whether in louche lounge, heartless hotel, classy club, ritzy restaurant, or once years ago on the wind-whipped corner of Buchanan and Argyle (as an American would have it), *al fresco* in the Scottish rain, tone and timing perfect, phrasing filled with a defiantly disconsolate Glaswegian finesse – the drunk with Sinatra's smile. The song then was *Some Enchanted Evening*. For so many enchanted evenings, I *thank* yesterday...

Act One

He was able to turn a thirty-two bar song into a three act play.

Julius La Rosa
on Frank Sinatra

ONCE OR TWICE

Once or twice I did it
I wish it had been more
Talent? Oh I hid it
Success is such a bore
I was patchily productive
Just lacked the will to win
Being self destructive
Does ambition in

The heart will hedge its bets
And nurse its small regrets
Like that first cocktail at noon
The dues you paid feel like debts
Showbiz welched on. Still who forgets
After hours Nat Cole sets
Or Crosby's crowd-pleaser croon

The final number of the night
The bar's about to close
A big finish? Right!
A slow one I suppose
Go out on a high
Take the bartender's advice
Fame passed me by
But I did it
Once or twice...

LEAVE RIGHT NOW
(AND STAY)

If you believe love long awaited
Isn't really fated
Leave right now
If the boy or girl next door
Starts to make you snore
Leave right now
If the eleven-o'clock number
Cannot rouse you from your slumber
Leave right now

But if a deftly danced duet
Set the second sweethearts met
Still has anything to say
Why don't you take your seat
Sample the bittersweet
(On Forty-Second Street)

And stay

What if the torch song's glow has faded
Rather than upbraided
Romantics should be serenaded
(Joints like this never get raided!)
No way

So... stay, stay, stay

But if happy ever after
Tends to crease you up with laughter
Leave right now
If you reckon one and only
Is just postponing being lonely
Leave right now

If the genre of love story
Is a phoney category
Best be on your way
But if your heart can still be melted
By a ballad being belted
In a cabaret
Check your fedoras and your furs
For an hour of his 'n' hers

And stay

WHERE MY HEART
SHOULD BE

If there was a clinic
You could visit as a cynic
And come out cured
Just walk in full of guile
And leave behind each wile
Emerging un-inured
I'd put my nature with its twist
On the waiting list
Except there's nothing they could do
To make me trusted or true
There's neither tincture nor tonic
To turn this Don Juan less sardonic

I'm not your Moon 'n' Junist
More an opportunist
Where there's a liberty to take
I'm a Restoration Rake!
Unlike in some happy, sappy ballad
My days were never salad
Instead of wedding bells
Too busy bedding belles

I'm a real hard case
In my breast there's a space
Where my heart should be
At the sound of sweet talking

I start walking
Footloose and fancy free
A roué, a rover
All over
That's me

SHOWTIME IS NO TIME
TO BE ALONE

Up goes the curtain
Up strikes the band
Down goes my luck
Like the drink in my hand
No co-star to kiss me
Or chorus to miss me
For all the curtain calls I've known
No audience to care
That I'm no longer there
Showtime
Is no time
To be alone

Just before eight
Is the moment I hate
When old troupers moan
Showtime
Is no time
To be alone

I've no fans to speak of
Memories recede
For eclipsed leading men
Life's tiresome to lead
Who cares that my phrasing
Was once thought trail-blazing

Back when the big-shots would phone
The booze helps me bear
All that's left there
Like a cracked LP spinning
At last I'm beginning
To try out my tenebrous tone

Showtime
Is no time
To be alone

No

You think that the spotlight won't fade
That life will be one long encore
At the matinee you've still got it made
By nightfall... no more

No

Showtime
Is woe-time
Oh
Never, no time

To be alone

FREE TO BE LONELY

Why be a schmuck?
Accept the good luck
Of one special person
Try a little trust
Go ahead just
Don't waste time rehearsin'
If you want my advice
Don't even think twice
Forget chapter 'n' versin'
Exes expunge
Please take the plunge
She's waiting for your call
Can't you see only
Being free to be lonely
Isn't any freedom at all
I came close once
She'd have said 'yes' in a minute
But love's dunce
Held her hand yet wouldn't win it
No maybe no might
She was so right
For me
But I let love pass
Greener grass
Alas
Restless me

I'm still free
Free to be lonely

Do I rue or regret
Sure, when the hours are small and wee
Other girls that I met
Meant much less to me
No *carpe florem* petal
Persuaded me to settle
Down; always one more to adore
For this troubled troubadour
Wistful he
Endlessly
Free to be lonely

If it really gets you here
Mostly it's because
I'm not the man I was
Old sorrows sear
As loves and wants
Give way to hates and haunts
And all the rest is fear
Until suddenly your pillow
Has become a weeping willow
And you count each tear
Till the dawn gets near

SHE THAT I SEEK

A homely honey
She that I seek
Should be feisty yet meek
In couture that's chic
Charming and funny
Just like Daddy's money
She won't look like my mother
She won't cook like my mother
Her chin won't be weak
So softly she'll speak
She that I seek

After finishing school
No! You fool
I said 'Finishing School'!
Somewhere top drawer
Bryn Mawr
As a Rule
(Though Radcliffe is 'cool')
Given her gene pool
As befits her breeding
Her bedside reading
Will be Hesse
Sure... Hermann
Yet *besser*
In the German!

Her that I'm after
Should have lady-like laughter
Though husky and low
A big no-no
Would be a cunning will drafter
Though as gold diggers go
I'm no gigolo
She'll be expertly pally
With the board of the Ballet
As every museum must see
Truly a trophy
Trustee
Three openings a week
For she that I seek

A demure debutante
With a moneyed maiden aunt
I'm gonna meet her how?
Not in this dive now
I can't I shan't
No not tonight
Under the pool table light
Of Bill's Bar & Grill, no
I don't guess I will so
The prospects are bleak
For finding her that I seek

SHOWSTOPPER TIME

Cameo rôles
Damned more souls
Than God the Father
Would I prefer the lead?
Why yes indeed
You bet I'd rather!
I'd sooner sing a hit
Than this slight silly bit
Since you inquire
But all I know is
It's death or showbiz
I'll never retire

You give all you've got
For that follow spot
You cut your capers
Your talent's the same
As when your name
Was in the papers
But now when your brief
Is comic relief
(Not even 'Comic Relief'...)
There's no high note clinch
Though if they but knew it
In my dreams I still do it
Could too at a pinch

Baritone heaven
Used to start at eleven
When the gal got her guy
Now I head home in a cab
While some kid has a stab
At making her cry
As I reminisce
About that curtain closer kiss
Back in my prime
I'd trade every payday
For just half a heyday
And showstopper time

SOMEDAY

Someday
I used to say
Someday
Some way
I'll find someone
Somehow

That was back then
Back when
Again
Wasn't
And again
Maybe one day
Needs to be now
O wow!

Am I in love
Well I don't know
Between pals
Can passion grow
When romance
Is just so-so?
A big no-no
Oh-oh

Twenty raindrops for each ray

I'm grimly going grey
Is this a course we two can stay
I really wouldn't care to say

Anyway
I just thought hey
Could someday
Be today
So if I may
And it's okay
Let's make today
Some day
Someday

IF UNFÊTED

Please understand
For each part I land
I stand indebted

Ageing egos get brittler
As each rôle's yet littler
We washed up have netted

But I sing out loud
An old pro and proud
If unfêted

A tiny tear
For my torched career
One eye wetted

THE TRUTH
WILL OUT

The cynic will bet
On a sound-stage sunset
As his way home he's wending
Yes you have to have faith
In that risible wraith
The cute happy ending
There's nothing arch or coy
About girl meets boy
In the musical theatre
Than the ears of corn
On a Kansas morn
Only a show tune's greater!

To credit the incredible
To believe in make-believe
Syrup too sweet to be edible
The truth out to deceive
By any honourable standard
God knows a standard has no standards at all
To the gods I've often pandered
With a cheap curtain call

Where's the truth
In star-crossed youth
On the Great White Way?
What isn't phoney

Is sheer baloney
Always was, still is, today
Oi vey!

A word to the wise
All those wonderful lies
Really come true
A high-kicking finish
Needn't diminish
What's in it for you

Guys who are gay
Put the broad in Broadway
Nothing's what it seems
Writers who are funny
Strictly for the money
Sell us our own sweet dreams

Every whisper is a shout
Each certainty a doubt
Mid-days mostly made of moonbeams
Girlish complexions got with greasepaint and creams
The truth will out

Though the facts may pout
The truth will out

I CAN SING

Boy is forty not my forte
Thirty was
Instead of sojourn or sortie
There's a shaky pause
When they request an interview
To hype whatever hokum's new
The print is small
What's a headliner's to do
When he knows he's nearly through
Be relieved to be working at all

Directors deem it strange
That my old three octave range
Remains intact
The rôles and costumes change
And the way I'm backed
Two synths, a jaded dep
Where once cool cats were hep
While an MD swayed
It's a has-been's Hobson's choice
If he wants to use his voice
And still get paid

For that glorious thing
Still to sing
I can sing

I can swing
Hear those high notes resounding
I emote
From the throat
And not just by rote
(Mustn't gloat)
Till every heart's pounding

Like Trenet in trenchcoat
And trilby
What forty's not, fifty will be!

I can sing

IN THE COCKTAIL HOUR

In the cocktail hour
Wonders can occur
Perhaps a whisky sour
Will appeal to her
After all an aperitif
Is but the beginning
To my amazement and relief
The martinis aren't winning
Though my head is spinning
From a lifetime's gin-ing
One's amatory powers
Survived a hundred happy hours –
Too many cocktail hours

An intimate old oak bar
An art deco shaker
So good so far
Where will you take her
Between six thirty and eight
Let drink decide your fate
With each olive you devour
Fewer demons lower
No Casanovas cower
In the cocktail hour

If tonight

Life's a fight
My friend throw it
For a toney lounge lit low
By a Tiffany lamp's golden glow
And patter that is smooth
In a cosy corner booth
Not too near the piano
Nor too far away, ah no
So the crooner's occult power
Fills that baby-grand bower
In the cocktail hour

Never's always now or
In the cocktail hour
Like an orchid that other indoor flower
Your martini's musky scent will wow her
In the cocktail hour

In the cocktail hour

LAST NIGHT'S GIRL

Last night's girl
You know I scarcely kissed her
I'm off balance I birl
I heard bagpipes skirl!
I wasn't home before I missed her
A sentimental lapse?
But what if perhaps
I was finally ready
To go (somewhat) steady
To give love a whirl
With last night's girl

My heart looped the loop
On her brownstone stoop
I wasn't asked up for a night-cap
And though her smile said more
Than an open door
I pecked her cheek
Misguidedly meek
Like a right sap

Last night's girl
I just walked her home
After that last chaste twirl
Will this tom-cat still roam
I suppose I'd planned

A one night stand
But hadn't the heart

Being smitten ain't smart
But I'll give it a whirl
With last night's girl

IF THE KEY
IS RIGHT

Cupid please
Why all those minor keys
Can't this affair be major
If some heart-throb needs your 'C's
I'll take your 'B's or 'D's or 'G's
Heed my pleas, please
To engage her
Like an old stager
Can't I open in Act Two
With a tune that isn't blue
The kind that gets the girl
Though I'm a hopeless height and age
To feature centre stage
Can't we give it a whirl

When you've struck a chord
And you're adored
You feel a duet coming
You're Manhattan's manor's lord
With an Academy award
Soon forthcoming
(For that duet they're humming)
No more melancholy tints
In minor, minor stints
No more ah- and um-ing
When agents suggest slumming

Get those guitars strumming
And trumpets tum-te-tumming
I feel a duet coming

So maestro if you will
I don't need to top the bill
Just write me one barnstormer
And if I sound over the hill
The orchestra can fill
Till my pipes get warmer
Yes I'll start the second act
With a performance that is packed
With youthful vibrancy and light
There'll be smiles and swoons and sighs
When we lovers harmonise
If the key is right

TONIGHT IS
TOMORROW TODAY

Dawn's hyacinth hue
The mist and the dew
That patch of pink in the blue
Means I have to leave you
Though lingering I grieve to

Tonight is tomorrow today

First light leaking in
The streetcar bell's din
Shaving soap on my chin
The paper-boy's grin
Living in sin
Let forever begin

Tonight is tomorrow today

Time didn't stand still
It was dancing
The hours needed no whiling away
We won't let daybreak's chill
Backward glancing
Stand in eternity's way

At what morning forbade
The songbirds aren't sad

Bluebirds bless *en ballade*
Each rapture we've had
Let your troubadour add
A minstrel's *aubade*

Tonight is tomorrow today

THIS QUIET LITTLE
QUARTER OF MINE

Just off Main Street
Anytown, garden front and rear
Picket fence included
Is where we won't meet
How dear! How drear
Commuters are deluded
One supposes
By the roses
Jimmy Stewart living right next door
The promised land denied to Moses
Kept pristine and green with hoses
And the latest luxury lawn mower

There, there; that's theirs
Who cares?

A studio apartment up several flights of stairs
The neighborhood not up and coming
Cold water plumbing
Ergo no yuppies slumming
Our Bohemian nose-thumbing
Enthrals the squares
No busybodies pry
Cops and candidates don't come by
The artist would be brave
Who established an enclave

From what is usually meant
By the term 'low rent'
It's a dizzying descent
The famished roaches rarely dine
The bars decline
To serve fine wine
Even Gertrude Stein
Would draw the line
Gaps in ev ry n on sign
But within a dozen blocks I pine
Quaint, it ain't
Yet how divine
This quiet little quarter of mine

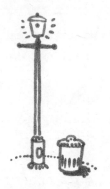

CARE
FOR ANOTHER?

A fool
On a stool
Will as a rule

Care for another

That kind of guy
Believes he can buy
A friend or a brother

Care for another?

Don't mind if I do
Who's caring for you?

Care for another?

Buddy I swear
You've got me there
Do I really dare

Care for another?

When as you can see
Having ordered three
I don't care for me

Surely that's clear
Like this martini here

Care for another?

For keeps
For good
She wishes I could

Care for another

Care for another?

BIGGER THAN EVER

There comes a moment in the jazz life
If one still has life
When you learn that what you thought was all your own
Was just a loan
When the only applicable hip requires replacing
When what you're facing
Is the unknown

Not walk-ons in Poughkeepsie
Or reduced to cabbing gypsy
But the big nada
Or the Saviour's Dada
If God had a Fada
Unless you wuz badda
Than you thought

When after all nine curtain calls
That sucker really falls
Despite one last encore
You've finally run through the whole store
Of more
There ain't no more
No more

Old stagers do not die
When they reach the end of the line

One matinee they dry
In the limelight's shine
No whimper no whine
And since memories stay bright
They make a comeback every night
Recordings endeavour
To make them bigger than ever

For the deceased
Sales have increased
Coffins box clever
For the dead life's a thread
Fate must sever
Go figure
I'll be bigger
Than ever

When after all nine curtain calls
That sucker really falls...

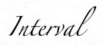

Interval

Act Two

Too many writers write self-pity. Audiences hate that in a character.

Jule Styne

THE SHOW'S GONNA
OPEN ANYWAY

When the hit they go home humming
Isn't actually forthcoming
And the show's gonna open anyway

Without the tune mailmen'll whistle
As they deliver each epistle
Of execution there'll be no stay

Finagle something fast
Ephemera that'll last
Something timeless, immemorial that keeps

Try adding to the canon
By hooking every fan on
That classic producers plan on
Without which no-one sleeps

In one's attempts to be inventive
Some insomniac incentive
Is the show's gonna open come what may

With a tune that panders, milks and caters
That you'll hear in elevators
That the backers want by yesterday

Because the show can't open any day

For the tryout out of town
We need a number of renown
So the show's gonna open like we say

Let's pray the muse is prompt tonight
With those first few bars we've yet to write
We've had it with here's hopin'
Where's the lyric we can rope in
While black coffee keeps us copin'
With the misery and mopin'
Turning night into day

'Cos the show's gonna open anyway!

BLAME YESTERDAY

I'm just calling to say
But I can't find the phrase
I was appalling today
And lots of other days
What I mean is
I don't mean to be mean
The thing about a has-been is
All his maybes have been
Always was always will be
Just what I'll still be

Me Me Me

Baby I guess
It's too late to confess
Anyway

I'm calling to own up
To not being grown-up
Just ringing to say
Hi Hello Hey
For the way I was today

Blame yesterday
For today
Blame yesterday

TRULY, REALLY,
HONESTLY

A part, a rôle
A heart that's whole
In terms a contradiction
The masks we wear
Feel real out there
To act
In fact
Means fiction
Why should it surprise you
If our lies are true
When your fulfilment is what we're wishin'
Ache relief
Through make-belief
A love
Above
Suspicion

This is me
But then so is he
And we're both on the level
You may put your trust
As maybe you must
In angel and devil
Love has to deceive
To let lovers believe
A metaphysical conceit

Marvell and Donne
Had truth on the run
Working both sides of the street
Ever constant till I leave you
Here's a pledge that you can cleave to
Sure as the sun that's above you
I truly, really, honestly, love you

Parlando
We all understand O
Semiotic sleight of hand O
Love's ludic ironies outfox
Post-modern paradox
Just take a deco
At Umberto Eco
So

A part, a rôle...

IF SHE'D
JUST CALL

Was it a one shot deal
She doesn't answer my calls
By now her hall's
Full of my letters
I confess in all candour
To deserving sauce for the gander
The venery boot
Is on the other foot
I've met my match in hard-to-getters
Or calming down
She's only out of town
Will be back in touch
Ring to say
Nothing much
O the interest girls pique
In less than a week
OK a day
After one day and night
My wicked ways I'll repent
Pledge to be a gent
No rivals in sight
No none, that's right
None at all
Playing playboy would pall

If she'd just call

YOU CAN'T ARRANGE YOUR LUCK

You learn the changes and the charts
How to write out all the parts
Suspend/ diminish
Piano fade/ big finish
The predictable the strange
Yet the vicissitudes of Fate
You can't orchestrate
No you can't arrange
Your luck
Riddle, Duke, Basie, May
Cats who really knew the score
How to grandstand
On the bandstand
Or tease out a tempo change
With the wave of a hand
Not even they...

When the trumpets should be mute
About that you are astute
Never troubled
By a bar line doubled
Or the woodwinds' range
Ah but destiny's date
You will never orchestrate
No you can't arrange
Your luck

WHERE THE HEART
STORES SUCH THINGS

How'd the dime fall
Did she finally call
Did she ever?
No... as in never!
Like that girl on the train
You don't see again
Don't say a word to
Whose 'my station' smile
Every once in a while
Still gets referred to
As the torch singer sings

Where the heart stows such things

When her call failed to come through
Did I maybe say 'phew'
To my little black book
My heart's off the hook
In love a newcomer
I simply mistook
A swallow for summer?
No I can honestly say
It wasn't that way
I miss her still
Always will
A little more each day...

In the reliquary there
With the dolour and despair
Of another doomed affair

Where the heart stores such things

With a skelf from the True Cross
A man must venerate his loss
Embellish and emboss
The song he sings

Where the heart hoards such things
Where the heart holds such things
Where the heart stores such things

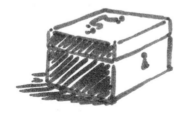

THE GODS PAY NO HEED

Writing songs
Isn't righting wrongs
Nor smiting throngs
The gods pay no heed
When you pen a lyric
The victory is pyrrhic
Inconsequence indeed
What a show-tune means
Is a hill of beans
Not Mount Parnassus
We scale the heights
Of opening nights
For Apollo to darn us

In Pan's pied-à-terre sir
You'll hear Fielding, Hart or Mercer
The more garrulous the terser
Harburg, droll Cole
Or his successor
Yorkville's ol'
Frank Loesser
The lyric *and* its air
Well that needs Irving Berlin's flair
Or Sondheim's; Steve's up there
With his elegant despair
On the Bible word-smiths swear

That it's fiendishly unfair
Still the deities don't care
Valhalla looks down upon
And Odin will frown upon
Even 'proper' poets
Thor's thunder ain't applaudin'
Wilbur, Nash, Wodehouse or Auden –
Bravo wits?
No it's
The Supreme Being being ratty
With the local literati

I'm not tipping Tin Pan Alley
To beat a sweet Socratic sally
Who'd claim a hoofer's knowledge
Nixes Harvard College
Agape doesn't come
With every hit you hum
At full throttle

Yet Aristotle
Is a half full bottle
As is Duns Scotus
Love's proven on the pulse
Of a ditty, deftly dulce
The Gershwins wrote us

THE GENIUS
OF GENE

Singin' in the Rain
Was on the tube again
Tinseltown tears are cheap
But I had a little weep
(Mind you have to factor in
The vermouth and the gin)
Gene making me regret
The girl I didn't get
Yet
Après the deluge
His raindance is still huge!

This one's for Gene Kelly
The working stiff's Astaire
Who needs suave or debonair
When you're ten feet in the air
He knew his place
Was in choreographed space
Boy! boxing meets ballet there

If you had the moves, the grace
The timing, the pace
The whole Ohio Irish bit
Plus endless supplies
Of twinkling eyes
And you were Olympically fit

If you held a tune a lit-
Tle shakily yet so securely
Whilst oozing sex appeal so demurely
But impurely!
You'd have half what on screen
Was the genius of Gene
In films that never pall
When song and dance could still enthral
His was vaudeville's last curtain call

The greatest hoofer of them all

LEARN TO
DANCE

If you want to get ahead with girls completely
Take a leaf or two out of my book
(Byways worth wending)
To knock 'em dead albeit sweetly
And discreetly
My technique might just be worth a look
(Patents pending)

Learn to dance!

Just a few steps
Waltzes, foxtrots, *schottishes*, tangos
Military two steps
Go quick, slow, slow
Where every fan goes
Leave nothing to chance
Nothing, not one thing, no no
To cha-cha chance
Eightsome reels
Pasos dobles, Polkas, pavannes
Each one appeals

Love's wallflower advance guard
Fills up her dance card
Learning the moves
To jack up his chances

He whom the ballroom behoves
By asking for dances
Learns half of romance is
The glides and the grooves

Learn to dance!

Preen, pirouette, pivot and prance
He who holds to happenstance
Too timid to advance
Will be looked at askance
For the *coeur*
Of amour
To be sure
Don't be demure
The pleasure
Is pure
It's gaucheness's cure

Learn to dance!

BLACK
& WHITE

A martini tastes much better
When you're not in some old sweater
Manhattans too
If you want to look top dollar
Try shiny shoes and a shawl collar
I promise you
This is true
(Of even you!)

You'll always feel at home
When you model monochrome
You can't go wrong
You don't believe I'm right?
Why it's there in black and white
A Cole Porter song

Yes satin and studs
Are dandy duds
For supper club jazz
No-one louche is low
If his tie's a bow
And has pizzazz

A chap's choice of evening wear
Fails to make him Fred Astaire
Who could cut that kind of dash?

Nor can merely being fond
Of black-tie, blameless on James Bond
Predispose one to panache

But every once in a while
I still stand by the style
Of my old d-j
That got worn and frayed
While dance bands played
The way they don't today

A tux's elegance and ease
Will flatter, slim and please
Picture Bogey running Rick's
So shoot those starched, linked cuffs
For there are very few rebuffs
Correct attire can't fix

REALLY
BLUE

I used to work aboard the liners
A de-luxe gig
I was distraction for the diners
In white tux rig
The dames showed their devotion
While the moon lit up the ocean
Whatever made them that way
Had less to do with Neptune
Than the hypnotic late-night hep tune
Swingin' dance-bands play

If they'd been booked on the Titanic
There would have been no panic
Those boys were iceberg cool
They never missed a beat
As I swept broads off their feet
By the swimming pool
(Well there as a rule)

I was a looker, loud and louche
A creep, a heel
Frequently farouche
The whole lounge lizard deal
Putting away a lot of Moët
A matelot Pal Joey
With bedroom eyes

Through all the action I was grabbin'
In one or other first class cabin
I kept crackin' wise

I never made much money
But the starboard deck was sunny
Besides I loved those songs
No-one asks for them today
So stow that memory away
Where it belongs
Have you noticed how
After midnight now
It gets really blue

I'm not just talking about the night
The quality of light
I mean inside you?
So you've seen it too –
My what we've been through!
One's fancy starts to rove
As things go kind of mauve
That mood that Miles and Duke and Strayhorn knew

Really blue

THE LIFE
YOU GIVE IT

As cocktail crooners do
I worked a room or two
No Jule Styne
But doing fine
Doing my best
For the dollar in the glass
I'd make a fairish pass
At any reasonable request

A hard luck story
About fading looks and glory
The passion less the pity
That's any songsmith's city
A whole rainbow made of blues
The bad times and the booze
The providence you choose

You don't learn a song
You earn
A song
By the life you give it

The one who plays it wrong
Will phrase
It wrong
Lacking the guts to live it

A CHANSON
MOOD

When November's foggy breeze
Drifts along the quays
I'm in a chanson mood
Another squalid, failed affair
Out of Kosmo and Prévert
In Maigret's neighbourhood
The soul of *chaque Parisien*
Is grey and sluggish as the Seine
A Satie *étude*

As an accordion grieves
Behind blue Gauloise smoke
That Camus bloke
Lost in autumn leaves
Would be overwrought
Quite distraught
In some *boîte*
Where the *plat* and plonk are cheap
And philosophising deep
L'ambience pas mal, quite good
I'm in a chanson mood

My accent *absolument* so-so
I'll confuse Verlaine and Rimbaud
Proclaiming Proust a prude
(The bits I understood)

From St Germain to Montparnasse
The attic skylight zone
For each footloose francophone
In the Closerie des Lilas
Or the Select I'll raise a glass
(With or without the wormwood)
A round Sam Beckett stood
Hemingway'd be here if he could
In a Juliette Greco interlude
Brumaire when Brel and Brassens brood

I'm in a chanson mood
A chanson mood

IN BERLIN

Circa nineteen thirty
Jokes were dissolute and dirty
Ja comedy was *kaiser*
Wunderbar to be a rhymer
In the vanguard that was Weimar
When Grosz was cracking wiser
To have been in *ein* review
Nein not with Kurt Weill who
Every bow, award and trick took
But Bert's other-other half Hanns Eisler,
No slouch with slick and sly slur
Who wrote the *Hollywood Songbook*

No place caught cabaret
Achh-oo!
Like Berlin in its day
Bless you!
Gesundheit!
The Nazi *zeit*
They got dead right

We're talking witty
Soon Broadway didn't have to soich
For talent that was Deutsch
In New Yoik City
I wish they'd hoid my pipes

In those expressionist kneipes
Where mood and moment meshed
Cigar and leather coat
Snarling the songs he wrote
The *geist* of Bertolt Brecht

The fat cats satire smote
Brecht

Echt Brecht

ARGENTINA CRIED

Somewhere in Buenos Aires
For daring dancers there is
A torrid tango bar
Down a sordid alley
Where illicit lovers dally
Under a southern star

Forget Evita!
Argentina cried
No tango poet lied
Every bandeón sighed
When Piazzolla died
Sex by any other name
Tunes no matador can tame
A macho ritual
Eyes and hearts aflame
One last Maradona game
The pitch'll
Never be the same

Forget Evita!...

The gaucho's rôle to glide her
His fierce black widow spider
Whose web has just got wider
Her hair flicks the floor

His heels they click and slide
He twists round at her side
Exuding pampas pride
He scoops her up once more

Forget Evita!...

Frankly a bordello
Soundtrack by Gardel, no
Suave and swarthy fellow
Will be denied a dance
And as the gramophone
Begins again its sultry moan
Risky romance
Is bought in advance
With one hot glance

LOVE LOVE LOVE

A guitar plucked idly
On a Rio beach
The chords of carnival in each
Bassy bossa nova to feat-
Ure love, love, love

Getz and Gilberto
Trading licks
A caipirinha mix
Old dogs with their new tricks
Si, see...
Love, love, love

Sad, sad, sweet, sad
Strings growl low
From Santa Monica
To Sao Paolo
The sax will yowl oh
Love, love, love

From London
Down to Lima
Every girl's from Ipanema
With Jobim a
Kid can dream a
Variation on a theme a

Dream, a dream, a
Dream of
Love, love, love

WHAT THE SAXOPHONE
KNOWS

When the shadows gather round
Midnight's sound
Is a blue horn blown
Tenor or baritone
A saxophone
The whole world's woes
That's what the saxophone knows

Wolves can wail
A banshee is bale-
Ful, but that hooting horn
Is so forlorn
You hear a heart being torn
Lost love's lows
Are what the saxophone knows

Despondency, despair
Wistful, wounded wisdom there
A soprano horn can howl
Like an owl
On the prowl
Or a gurning ghoul
Misery in theory
Should never sound so eerie
As those keys disclose
What the saxophone knows

IF IT WASN'T
FOR THE HAT

On a sidewalk that's wet
Cupping a cigarette
Back-lit by a street lamp's arc
Sighing over sorrows
And that last dime fortune borrows
That's a blues you're whistling in the dark
Your trenchcoat's belted
And your collar's up
Her heart's unmelted
She doesn't care to sup
But what an attitude you strike
Just what the lovelorn should look like
Yet the whole thing would fall flat
If it wasn't for the hat

A returning vet
A film noir vignette
Triple crossed by a widow with a veil
She can stitch 'em
She can ditch 'em
Even Robert Mitchum!
You're one melancholy outmanoeuvred male

But at least you have a hat
A brim to snap
A fedora at that

(Not a cap
Like a sap
Would doff to a toff)
Hats even look good when taken off
To snarl 'you dirty rat'
Cagney had to have a hat

If it wasn't for the hat

LIFE'S
NO CABARET

My romance never took
Life lacks lyrics and a book
Its finale's more gruesome than grand
What on stage cheers you up
Off it, tears you up
Oh the act
We call fact
Should get panned

Whatever Ebb and Kander say
Life's no cabaret
The heart I wear on my tuxedo sleeve
Must never reveal
What I truly feel
Beyond the stage door
I'm lonely once more
Still Broadway's the best way to grieve

A radical rewrite
Won't redeem love's last night
The producer's not the Creator
The forty-second-street feel-good factor
Takes its bow with the actor
Until tonight I never knew
Love's only ever true
In musical theatre

I'M SINGING

I'm not in a show
Won't be again I know
But I'm singing

Perhaps you will excuse it
If suddenly I lose it
Because... I'm singing

There's no first-night crowd to hear
And no last-act hit to cheer
An encore for yesteryear, well I'm singing

The top notes may have flown
From my 'fruity' baritone
But I'm singing

Though my phrasing's pretty pure
My breathing's less secure
Yet... I'm... singing!

If I ain't half as di-a-phragm-my
Hell these days I'm twice as hammy
WHEN I'M SINGING

My esteemed glissando glide
May be somewhat on the slide

Still I'm singing

And when fickle fans forgot
Could it be
That she
Did not?

Ever after, who'd have thought

A love song's what
I'm singing

ONCE OR TWICE
(REPRISE)

Once or twice I did it
I wish it had been more
Talent? Oh I hid it
Success is such a bore
I was patchily productive
Just lacked the will to win
Being self destructive
Does ambition in

The final number of the night
The bar's about to close
A big finish? Right
A slow one I suppose
Go out on a high
Take the bartender's advice
Fame passed me by
But I did it once or twice

Once or twice I did it...

GOOD NIGHT
(EXIT MUSIC)

Good night
Drawn drapes
Good night
Opera capes
Good night
Maestri
Good night
(Buy the CD!)
Good night

Good night
And how
Good night
A final bow
Good night
Go home
Good night
(Close this tome)
Good night

Bravo encore
Can't ask for more
You know the score
Autographs at the stage door
Good night
Good night